S0-AYT-665

THE IRRITATED OYSTER

&
OTHER OBJECT LESSONS FOR CHILDREN

HARVEY D. & PATSIE A. MOORE

ABINGDON PRESS
NASHVILLE, TENNESSEE

THE IRRITATED OYSTER AND OTHER
OBJECT LESSONS FOR CHILDREN

Copyright © 1976 by Abingdon Press

All rights reserved
No part of this book may be reproduced in any manner
whatsoever without written permission of the publisher
except brief quotations embodied in critical articles
or reviews. For information address Abingdon Press,
Nashville, Tennessee.

Library of Congress Cataloging in Publication Data

ISBN 0-687-19690-6

MOORE, HARVEY DANIEL, 1942-
   The irritated oyster and other object lessons for children.

   SUMMARY: Brief stories illustrate Christian values and princi-
ples.
   1. Children's sermons. 1. Sermons. 2. Christian life I. Moore,
Patsie, Ann, joint author. II. Title.
BV4315.M6237   248'.82   75-30886

Scripture quotations are from the Revised Standard Version of the
Bible, copyrighted 1946, 1952, and 1971, by the Division of Christian
Education, National Council of Churches, and are used by
permission.

MANUFACTURED   BY   THE   PARTHENON   PRESS   AT
NASHVILLE, TENNESSEE, UNITED STATES OF AMERICA

This book is dedicated to:

        Patti
        Daniel
        David
        &
        Nikki

Four beautiful reasons for living close to God.

CONTENTS

THE IRRITATED OYSTER

PREFACE

When I first began sharing with children in the morning worship service, I had no idea of the special place this experience would come to hold in the hearts of the total congregation, regardless of age. Recently, during the celebration of the Week of the Laity, I had an opportunity to sit as a part of the congregation. As the time for the children's sermon grew near, it was a source of joy to see the children throughout the sanctuary begin to stir with anticipation. As I watched the young high school girl relate the object lesson, I could see afresh why this approach has such great power and meaning to those who participate in it.

First of all, it is *fun!* That may surprise some people, but it is, in fact, just that. The person giving the lesson gets a chance to sit down on the steps and be *with* the children. The children themselves have an opportunity to come down the aisle and relax with one another and to share in an open give-and-take relationship with the minister. It is not at all unusual for all of us to have a good laugh or smile as a part of the talk. Learning about Jesus is a happy experience, and if we speak of joy, I see no harm or irreverence in sharing some.

Second, it is *relevant*. The objects that are selected are, for the most part, taken from the daily experiences of the children. They can be readily identified in the talk itself and can relate in the weeks following. The more an object is a part of the child's world, the more frequently he will recall and relate the idea you have related to him. Consequently, the faith itself will come to be more real.

Third, it is *simple*. The greatest aspect of Christ's teaching method was his ability to translate the most difficult and abstract concepts into the simplest of terms.

Last, and possibly most important, is the inclusion of the children in the process of the talk. I believe that the talk should be well thought out, but not rigid in its presentation. It has been my experience that if the children are allowed to take the lead, they will virtually "preach" the message themselves. In fact, it is not unusual for some of them to see the point immediately and then do an excellent job of relating it to the others. I encourage this type of group and peer conversation.

When the children leave the chancel, they are aware that they have been involved *in* an experience rather than talked to.

One last comment should be made concerning the openness of the conversation. In any give-and-take situation, especially where concepts are involved, there will be varying opinions. It is essential in my opinion that the child's viewpoint be respected. If he expresses an opinion or feeling that does not coincide with the thrust of the message, it should be remembered that the child is more important than the talk.

8

We are not here to perform, but to build relationships and demonstrate Christian love and acceptance. One incident of accepting a child's disagreement or opinion may accomplish a great deal more than all the sermons combined.

There is no greater reward than having the children know that they can state freely what they think and feel and still be accepted as persons of equal value. It shares the most powerful message of all, and that is that God loves us, even as we are.

THE IRRITATED OYSTER

Text: *Ephesians 4:2-3. With all lowliness and meekness, . . . with forbearing one another in love, eager to maintain the unity of the Spirit in the bond of peace.*

Object: *A small rock and a pearl.*

Main Thrust: *Make an effort to respond positively to irritation.*

Can you all see this? (Hold the small stone in the palm of your hand.) It's very small, but I want all of you to take a good look at it. Now, you wouldn't think that something this small could cause much of a problem would you? But it can. And lots of times it does! How many of you have ever gotten a small rock like this one inside your shoe? (Let them have a show of hands and relate the experience.) It really can be a problem can't it? Every time you take a step it hurts. It rubs against your foot and pretty soon you have a very sore spot.

What is usually the first thing you do when you get a rock in your shoe and begin to feel it rubbing? That's right. You take off your shoe and throw the rock away. That solves the problem. Have you ever thought, however, what would happen if you could not take your shoe off? What if that rock just had to stay there? That could really be a very painful experience. Yet that is exactly what happens to poor Mr. Oyster.

How many of you know what an oyster is? Well, it's a kind of mollusk that looks like a little muscle, and it lives inside a shell at the bottom of the ocean. One of the biggest problems in an oyster's life is that sometimes a small grain of sand gets inside its shell, like the little rock that gets into your shoe. The oyster's problem is that it does not have any way of getting the sand out. It just stays there and rubs against him. It irritates him and makes him sore. That would be a hard way to go through life, wouldn't it? What do you think the oyster does? Can any of you guess? (At this point some of the ideas may prove interesting.)

Let me tell you what he does. When that rock starts rubbing and hurting, the oyster puts a very fine coating of fluid over it. The oyster is small, so he can only put a little on at a time, but every time that rock hurts him, he puts on a little more and a little more. Very slowly all the rough edges of that stone get smoothed out as it is coated over and over again. Do you know what finally happens? We get one of these. (Show them the pearls.)

They really are pretty, aren't they? You see, with a lot of patience and hard work, the oyster turns that painful rock into a beautiful smooth pearl. It isn't easy, but I'm sure you will all agree it is worth it in the end.

I think you can all see the lesson we can learn from the oyster. I don't mean that we are going to make the rocks in our shoes turn to pearls, but there is something more important than that involved. There are certain people in all our lives who affect us a lot like a rock in a shoe. They are the folks we just can't seem to get along with. They irritate us. Right? And how do we usually react to them? We are usually grumpy or we argue with them. We just don't get along at all. That is where we can learn from this pearl. Jesus said we ought to make a special effort to win over the people we have problems with, and that is what the oyster does.

This week, whenever someone does something that would make you angry or hurt your feelings, remember what Jesus said and return good things for bad and love for hurt. It is just possible that after a little while you will discover that your friendship has turned a rock into a pearl. It might just be a lot of fun to try.

READING YOUR MAIL

Text: *Joshua 1:6-8. Be strong and of good courage; for you shall cause this people to inherit the land which I swore to their fathers to give them. Only be strong and very courageous, being careful to do according to all the law which Moses my servant commanded you; turn not from it to the right hand or to the left, that you may have good success wherever you go. This book of the law shall not depart out of your mouth, but you shall meditate on it day and night, that you may be careful to do according to all that is written in it; for then you shall make your way prosperous, and then you shall have good success.*

Object: *Letter in an unopened envelope.*

Main Thrust: *If someone loves us enough to write, we ought to be willing to read the letter.*

I am really excited today. I have something with me that I have been waiting for for weeks. Can you see what it is? That's right, it's a letter. It is not just any letter; this is a letter from my father. How many of you have ever received letters from someone you loved? Hold up your hands. Oh, that's good. (You may want to let some of the children share their enthusiasm about birthday cards, etc.)

I do want to tell you one more thing about this letter. Remember I told you I have been waiting for it. Well, I have been waiting because I have some very difficult decisions that I need to make, and I wanted my father's advice and help. Now he has sent me this letter. Isn't that great? Do you know what I'm going to do with it? (You should get some obvious answers at this point like "Open it." If so, look surprised.) No, I'm not going to do that. I'm going to set it on our coffee table in the living room. I have a place all cleared off, and I am going to pass it every day and look at it and see how nice it looks there. Doesn't that sound like a good idea? No? Why not? You think I am supposed to read it! Well, I'm not so sure about that. Reading it would take time, and I'm very busy, you know. No, I think I'll just set it in the middle of the table and glance at the envelope now and then. That ought to be enough to let my dad know how much I think of what he says. What do you think?

(At this point you should get a chorus of responses letting you know they think it is nonsense.)

I don't really understand. You all disapprove of what I am planning to do with this letter. You say that if I really loved and respected my father and wanted his help I would open the letter and read it and then do what he says, not just place it unopened on a table and look at it. Is that what you're saying?

May I ask you one last question? If we feel that way about the letter, shouldn't we feel the same way about God's letters to us? Have you ever noticed what we do with our Bibles? We get them and tell everyone how

15

much we love God and how we respect his Word, but then we do exactly what I was just talking about. We place it carefully on a coffee table and never open it. It becomes a nice decoration, but hardly a guide for living. What do you think that tells God about how we feel?

This week, every time we get the mail, let's remember God's letters to us and take some time to read them. He loves us, and he is trying to guide us to a happy life now and an eternal life with him. Let's read a little bit each day and see what wonderful things he says.

DO MY ACTIONS SHOW IT?

Text: *James 2:8. If you really fulfil the royal law, according to the scripture, "You shall love your neighbor as yourself," you do well.*

Object: *A picture of my pet.*

Main Thrust: *If I love my pet I will take care of it.*

I have a picture with me this morning, and I would like all of you to have a chance to see it. I'll pass it around in a second. You will see that it is a snapshot of a dog. He's a pretty dog and a lot of fun to play with. His name is Tony and I really love him. In fact, anyone who has ever seen us together knows that I really love my dog. Of course, some folks do get confused about it. You see, I don't feed my dog. I don't give him any water. I let someone else do that, I'm too busy. I don't play with him and I don't want him to bother me except when I'm in the mood for him. When he's sick I just want him to go off somewhere where he won't bother me until he feels better. And you may be able to guess that I never pet him or tell him he's a good dog. So you can all see how much I really love him. He's my favorite dog. Can't you see how much I love him?

(At this point the children should be more than

ready to explain to you that you are acting in anything but a loving manner. Allow them time to express their thoughts.)

Some of you seem to have doubts about how much I love my dog. I really can't understand that. I *told* you I love him. Isn't that enough? It's not? What else do I need to do? (You may want to listen to some of the suggestions being offered.)

What I hear you telling me is that just *saying* I love my dog isn't enough. I have to *act* as if I love him as well. Is that what you mean? Oh, I think I understand. You are concerned more with what I do than with what I say!

In that case, let me make a suggestion. The same thing is true when we are talking about how we feel about people. Lots of times, especially in church, we will hear people say, "I love so-and-so." Or we may say "I love you" to someone who is close to us. But what about our actions? If we say we love someone and then refuse to help them, or say we like them and then snub them, what are we really saying?

Someone once said actions speak louder than words. That is something we ought to remember. This week whenever we find ourselves starting to say how much we love a person or what a good friend he is, let's pause for just a second and ask ourselves what we have done lately to demonstrate that love. In fact, why not set a goal. Try doing one good thing for each friend each day. Then we won't have to tell people we love them, they will know it by the way we act.

CATS AND DOGS

Text: *Matthew 5:43-45. You have heard that it was said, "You shall love your neighbor and hate your enemy." But I say to you, Love your enemies and pray for those who persecute you, so that you may be sons of your Father who is in heaven; for he makes his sun rise on the evil and on the good.*

Object: *A cat and dog or a picture of them eating out of the same bowl.*

Main Thrust: *We often think we have to have a person as an enemy when we can have him as a friend with a little effort.*

Have you ever heard the expression "They fight like cats and dogs"? How many of you have heard that before? How many of you have even seen a cat and a dog fight? Boy, they really get after each other don't they? We have a dog in our neighborhood that chases cats all over the block. Sometimes he will run the full length of the block just to bark at a cat. Of course, it's not always the dog's fault. We had a cat once that used to sneak up on the dogs and scratch them then run as fast as he could for a tree. I guess cats and dogs just don't get along. Do you think maybe that's just the way it is and there's nothing we can do to change it? (Get some responses and stories. Children like to talk

19

about their pets.) Well, lots of folks do feel that way, not only about cats and dogs, but about many other things in life as well.

If you will gather around a little bit, I have something in this box that I want you to see. I'll just reach in and here it is—a puppy. (Female pups are usually better for this type of talk.) She's quite a little dog, isn't she? Can you imagine what she would do if she saw a cat? It's a good thing there aren't any around. (Allow several children to agree. Some may even want to relate a recent dog-cat battle that they witnessed. Let them take part and make the point.)

Let me show you what else I have in the box. (Bring out the cat.) That surprises you doesn't it? A dog and a cat in the same box and they weren't fighting. In fact, if I put them down together now, you can see they get along rather well. They even like each other. What do you think about that? Here we all thought they would fight, and instead they are friends.

Now I should tell you that they didn't start out that way. In fact at first they didn't like each other very much. But as the three of us spent time together I managed to convince them that they didn't have to fight at all. They can share the same food dish, water dish, and even play together and not have any problems. You can see that with your own eyes.

But, can you see what we ought to learn from all this? Lots of time we will hear folks say that certain people are just natural enemies, like cats and dogs. They will never get along, no matter what. But that doesn't have to be the case, does it? We can see now that if we are willing to take a little bit of time and energy and get people to know one another, they really don't have to fight and might possibly even become friends.

This week, whenever you are tempted to get angry at someone, like a dog going after a cat, stop and remember these two friends, and remind yourself of one important thing. It's better to have a friend than an enemy. It may take longer to make a friend, but we all know it's worth it in the end. Let's work on that this week.

COMPLETE TRUST

Text: *Romans 8:35-39. Who shall separate us
from the love of Christ? Shall tribulation,
or distress, or persecution, or famine, or
nakedness, or peril, or sword? As it is
written,*

> *"For thy sake we are being killed all
> the day long;
> we are regarded as sheep to be
> slaughtered."*

*No, in all these things we are more than
conquerors through him who loved us. For I
am sure that neither death, nor life, nor
angels, nor principalities, . . . nor powers,
nor height, nor depth, nor anything else in
all creation, will be able to separate us from
the love of God in Christ Jesus our Lord.*

Object: *A child.*

Main Thrust: *Learn to trust God especially in difficult
situations, even death.*

I am going to need a special assistant this morning,
so I have asked Patti to help me. You can all see that I
have asked her to stand on the piano bench, and she
has her back to us. Now, what would happen if she
began to lean over backwards, farther and farther?
That is right, she would fall and probably get hurt. It
would really be a dangerous thing to do.

Now I am going to put a blindfold on Patti so she cannot see me, and I am going to ask her to stand very straight and then I want her to lean backwards until she falls. What do you think will happen? Right, if she does it she is going to get hurt. Would any of you like to try it? No? You don't want to get hurt either, is that it? Well, that makes sense. But, what if I told you that when Patti falls I am going to catch her? Do you think that would help? Remember, she can't see me, and she only has my word for it that I will not let her fall. Let's see what happens.

(Have the child remain very straight and slowly tip backward until she falls. For full effect she should keep her hands in her pockets. You should catch her just before she hits the floor. Obviously such an exercise should be practiced several times in advance. If done correctly it will have a tremendous effect on the children.)

What do you think of that? You think it could be pretty scary? Why? (The children will suggest several reasons, such as the fact that they could be hurt, the blindfold means they can't see, and various other things.)

With all those things to worry about, why do you think she did it? She didn't seem to be afraid? That's right! Even though she couldn't see me, she knew I was there and that I would catch her. She just relaxed and did her part, and she knew I would do the rest.

The point I really want to make this morning is that we should learn to trust God even more than Patti just trusted me. We can't see God, but we learn to trust him. There will be times when we feel like we are in lots of trouble or that we have problems that seem so big that nothing can help. That is when we remember God loves us, and if something happens, he is always there to catch us and help us back to our feet. God loves us, and he would never do anything to hurt us!

The next time you really have problems and it seems that everything is so hard to understand, that is the time to remember that God is always there to catch us, no matter what the problem might be. As much as I love Patti and want to protect her, God loves her even more. Just think how safe that makes her and all of us. God will always love us, and as long as we trust and obey him we need never be afraid of anything!

TALKING TO GOD

Text: *I Corinthians 13:1. If I speak in the tongues of men and of angels, but have not love, I am a noisy gong or a clanging cymbal.*

Object: *Tape recorder.*

Main Thrust: *If we repeat ourselves over and over in the same fashion in prayer, God may think we are not very serious about what we are saying.*

This morning I have a tape recorder, and it has a very special message for you. Would you like to hear it? Good! (The tape is of a boy's or girl's voice repeating over and over again the phrase, "Hi! I like you. Hi! I like you. Hi! I like you." Let the tape run until the children begin to get restless.)

Aren't you excited about what he is saying? You look a little bored. Are you tired of hearing the same thing over and over again? It does get a little dull doesn't it? What would you think if you had a friend who said almost exactly the same thing to you every time you saw him? Would you think he was sincere or just talking from habit? Right. You wouldn't be very impressed would you?

Have you ever wondered if God feels that way about prayers? I know some people who pray almost exactly the same prayer every night at the dinner table. In fact, it sounds a lot like that recording we just heard. No thought, just habit. Repeating the same thing just to get by. Do you think God notices that? Of course he does. How do you think it makes God feel to have us pray by habit and never give it any thought? (At this point you can pick up on all kinds of tremendous observations from the children.)

If we all agree that that is really not the best way to pray, what do you think we can do to change it? Right. David has a great idea! Let's talk to God as if he were right next to us and tell him how we really feel. Then we will be talking *with* him and not just be a recording talking *at* him. He likes that, and we will begin to realize how close he really is.

WHICH WOULD YOU CHOOSE?

Text: *Philippians 3:13-14. Brethren, I do not consider that I have made it my own; but one thing I do, forgetting what lies behind and straining forward to what lies ahead, I press on toward the goal for the prize of the upward call of God in Christ Jesus.*

Object: *A paper cup full of rocks and a few pieces of candy.*

Main Thrust: *Giving up old habits and replacing them with God's will is not a sacrifice, it is a joy.*

As you can see, I have a paper cup with me this morning, and I also have a pail of rocks. They're not very valuable rocks; in fact, I picked them up in the parking lot just before church. But I am going to do something with them. I am going to give them to Daniel. I would like him to take this cup and fill it up. You can have all you can put in the cup. (Give the child time to fill up his cup. You may want to comment on how nice some of the stones look and how happy he will be with them.)

That's good. Now you have a full cup. Before you sit down, there is one other thing. Can you see what I have in this box? Right! Candy! It sure does look good, doesn't it? I'll sample it and let you know. (Eat a piece and make sure everyone knows how good it is. You may offer some to one of the other children and let him comment on how good it tastes.)

Daniel, I'll tell you what. You may have some candy if you would like some. Wait, before you take any, I want to add one thing. You may only take as much candy as you can carry in that cup you have. I think that is going to be a problem. Your cup is already full. I guess there's nothing we can do. (It shouldn't take Daniel long to figure out the obvious. If he doesn't however, you can ask some of the other children for suggestions. They will be more than ready to offer them. Then he will begin taking the rocks out of his cup to make room for the candy.)

What are you doing? Why are you taking the rocks out? Oh, I don't want you to give up your rocks, that would be a real sacrifice. Are you sure you want to do that? Why? (He should be more than willing to tell you!) Of course, the candy is better than a few rocks. (As soon as Daniel begins emptying his cup give him *one* piece of candy and thank him. Otherwise you will have to give him a cupful and that usually does not please Mother. At this point you take the cupful of rocks and begin to make your point.)

As all of you just saw, Daniel had to make a choice. He knew he could have whatever he could put in his cup, but his cup was full before he knew about the candy. All he had to do to get the candy in the cup was toss out some rocks. The more rocks he threw out the more room he had for candy. Right? Do you think he was making a terrible sacrifice by throwing out the rocks? No? Why not? (You will get some of your best material at this time.) Of course. It's not a sacrifice if you're getting something better!

Let me explain just one more thing because it is something many of us have a hard time learning. All of us have lives just like this cup. They are ours to fill up any way we want. But, they will only hold so much. Once our time or our lives are filled up, then we have to make a choice if we want to put something else in. Most of the time our lives are full of rocks. Not bad things, but things we are just in the habit of carrying around. Then one day God offers something really good. He says, "Take some of these (hold up candy) and put them in your life." But we say, "No, I can't, my cup is already full." But the more we look at it, the more we know that what he is offering is better than what we have, so what do we do? That's right. We begin *making* room. It's not a sacrifice, it's a joy. We are giving up things we don't need to make room for something really good.

I want you to think a lot about that cup. Then, this week, whenever you find yourself with a choice between doing what God would want you to do—like helping someone or sharing or just going your own way—remember the cup. Maybe that is God's way of trying to offer you something better! Don't say your time is too full, make a little room to help. Then you'll see how really good it is to feel close to God.

A LITTLE EFFORT

Text: *Matthew 7:7-8. Ask, and it will be given you; seek, and you will find; knock, and it will be opened to you. For every one who asks receives, and he who seeks finds, and to him who knocks it will be opened.*

Object: *A large sack and several small toys.*

Main Thrust: *You get out of something what you put into it.*

I have a large paper sack with me this morning and several toys. Patti, would you please come up and be my helper today? I would like you to pick out some of the toys and place them in the sack please. Very good! She has selected four of them, and there are still five or six left. Now would you take the sack with you and have a seat again please. (Give her time to get settled in with the other children.)

Now, Patti, would you take out the airplane. (Name one of the toys she selected.) That sure is a pretty plane isn't it? Now would you take out the boat please. (Name another toy that she selected.) That's quite a combination. Now would you take out the football please. (This is one that she did not select.) What? You don't have a football? But you have to have a football, that is the toy I want to talk about. Look again. It

*you get out of the
Sack what you
put into it —*

...Why isn't it
...) I see, you
...ht, go ahead
...hy are you
...s sort of silly
...ng out of a sack that
you didn't put into it. That's right!

Now I would like you to really think about that for a moment. There is a saying that most of you have heard, and now you have seen it demonstrated. Do you know what it is? You get out of something what you put into it. That is true not only of sacks, but of just about everything in life. If you go to a good movie but you aren't willing to open your eyes, you shouldn't complain because you don't see anything, should you? No! If you don't want to put even that much effort into it, then you won't get anything out of it.

Do you know the same thing is even true of school? If you go and just rest and put nothing into learning, then you are going to get nothing back. It won't be the teacher's fault, it will be yours. In fact, that same thing is even true of Sunday school and church. When I was a little boy I would sometimes sit and draw pictures and play on the back pew. Do you know what I had when church was over? Scribbles and that was all. That was all I had put into it and that was all I got out of it. The other children would talk about enjoying different parts of the service, but I didn't know what they meant because I hadn't listened.

So this week, wherever you are or whatever you are doing, remember to do it well and try to get the most

31

from things by putting a real effort into it. You will get out of school, church, or playing just what you put into it. If you try, you will get a great deal because all of you have a lot to offer, and you will be rewarded. Let's try it and see what happens.

SLOWLY BUT SURELY

Text: *I Corinthians 1:18. For the word of the cross is folly to those who are perishing, but to us who are being saved, it is the power of God.*

Object: *A series of pictures of the sun rising.*

Main Thrust: *We often come to meet Jesus gradually.*

How many of you have ever taken a picture? Good! It's a lot of fun isn't it? I have a series of pictures here that I took from the office window. Each morning while I am reading I get a chance to see the sun come up. I have the pictures spread out here on the board, and I would like you to look at them very carefully. (Let them study the pictures for a few minutes.) Do you notice something of interest? The sun doesn't just *pop* up. You can see it comes up steadily but rather slowly. You may also notice that in those first pictures it is light even before the sun actually appears. In fact, it is rather difficult to say *exactly* when it does get light. But that doesn't mean it isn't happening, does it?

What I would like you to think about is that sometimes our experiences with God are just like this. Sometimes we feel that unless we can pick an exact time when God appears in our lives, then we haven't really met him; but that isn't true. Many times God comes into our lives the same way the sun comes up. A little light breaks in one place and then another, and very gradually he becomes more and more a part of our lives until eventually he is the most important thing we have.

So let's not worry about how fast God comes, let's just be glad that he comes and that he loves us.

THE SMOOTHING PROCESS

Text: *Proverbs 15:1.*
A soft answer turns away wrath,
but a harsh word stirs up anger.

Object: *Several rocks—some rounded and smooth and others rough.*

Main Thrust: *Soft answers can accomplish powerful things.*

I would like you to take a good look at this rock. It is about as hard and rough a rock as you will find anywhere. Go ahead and pass it around and let everyone take a good look at it. You can feel how rough and hard it is. While you're looking I am going to sip some water. (Let the children take a few seconds to pass the rock around.)

Now I wonder if you could give me some help. You have all seen how hard the rock is, but what I want is a smooth rock. How can I get this one smooth? Does anyone have a suggestion? (Such things as files, sandpaper, or even steel wool may be suggested. Accept each idea and explain the difficulties involved such as a file leaving marks, etc. When the children begin to run low on ideas produce the smooth stone.)

This is how I want the rock to look. Can you see this one? It is very smooth with not a mark on it. There are no file scratches or anything else. What do you think was used on *this* rock? Would you believe—water? That's right; just water. We were all trying to think of something rough or powerful enough to cut a hard substance when all the time it was water that could do it. I found this smooth rock on the beach near the ocean. The water had passed over it millions of times very slowly, but very definitely changing its shape by taking off the rough edges. In fact, if you ever get near the ocean you can see the high rough cliffs, then you can let some of the ocean water run through your fingers. Yet, it is the water that gradually shapes the cliff.

I think we can learn something about people from these rocks. We all know several boys or girls who are like this first rock. They have some rough edges. It might be a bad temper, or they may not be willing to share with others. It could be any number of things. When we see them we wonder what actions or words we can use that would be hard enough to knock off some of those edges. That is when we should remember the water and how it slowly molds and shapes rather than pounds like a hammer.

We can use that soft approach with people. We call it *love!* It doesn't mean we don't want them to change, it just means we are going to show them how they should be. Jesus said to return good for evil. If we return evil for evil, then we have been changed by the wrongdoers. We should all remember to return good for bad. But there is one other thing to remember about the water. It never stops. That's the secret. If it tried for a little while and then gave up, all the rocks would still be rough. The water *never* stops. That is how we must be. When we find someone with some rough edges, and we try to show him a better way, let's never get discouraged. It may take a long time, but gradually, with enough love, like water, his shape will begin to change. Let's try it and see.

WHAT DO YOU MEAN?

Text: *Ephesians 4:23-24. And be renewed in the spirit of your minds, and put on the new nature, created after the likeness of God in true righteousness and holiness.*

Object: *A live parakeet.*

Main Thrust: *One can learn to repeat things without knowing the real meaning.*

I have a real surprise for you today. How many of you know what it is? Yes, it's a bird, but what kind of bird? That's right, a parakeet. He's a very nice parakeet. He is very intelligent also. Listen for a second and let's see if I can get him to talk. (Give it a try. The more you can get the bird to repeat the same phrase over and over the more helpful it is.)

There, you see? He can talk just as clearly as can be. There are a great many things that he can say. Have any of you ever had a bird of your own that could talk? If you have then you know how to train birds. (Allow the children to share experiences.) But for those of you who have never had one I want to explain it. It is very simple actually. You just pick the phrase or sentence that you want the bird to learn, and then you repeat it to him over and over again. For a while it won't seem to be accomplishing anything, but if you do it long enough and keep repeating the same thing over and over, all of a sudden, one day he will be talking back to you. Then in a very short time he will be saying all sorts of things back to you. It really is a lot of fun.

After a while, however, you will begin to notice something interesting. The bird talks, but he doesn't really think like we do. What he actually does is listen and repeat. In other words, he talks but he doesn't understand what he is saying. That is what we mean when we say someone is "parroting" things. He is talking, but he is only repeating what he has heard and really doesn't understand it.

Sometimes that is what happens to people, especially in church or school. We want to learn about the Bible, for example, but we get sidetracked. We memorize verses or sentences, and that is good. But too often we stop there, and that can be a problem. If we stop at that point we are being just like the little bird. We have learned to repeat things, but we don't know what they mean. Let's remember the *meaning* is what is important.

Here is what I would like you to do this week. Each day as you study the stories from the Bible, think about what is being said. You should try to remember the stories, but if you hear something you don't understand or even that you don't agree with, speak up and ask questions. The important thing is not just to repeat, but to know *why* God says and does the things he does.

Remember, the better we understand a person the

more we can know and love him, and the more we can be loved. That is what God wants us to do. To know him and to love him so we can learn how much he loves us. Let's not just *repeat* his Word. Let's strive to truly understand it! Once we really understand it, then it becomes a part of us and we begin to live the kind of life Jesus talked about. We do it in a natural way that feels good to us and is great for others as well.

THE PERFECT GUIDE

Text: *Hebrews 12:1-2. Therefore, since we are surrounded by so great a cloud of witnesses, let us also lay aside every weight, and sin which clings so closely, and let us run with perseverance the race that is set before us, looking to Jesus the pioneer and perfecter of our faith, who for the joy that was set before him endured the cross, despising the shame, and is seated at the right hand of the throne of God.*

Object: *A plastic ruler with the letter guides in the center and a large piece of paper.*

Main Thrust: *A perfect guide gives perfect copies.*

I am going to need some assistance today. Here is what I would like you to do. Will you come up to this large sheet of paper and draw a straight line. Then on the straight line write the word *God*. David, would you do that please? (Let several of the children try. Most of them will just be learning to write, so it will be quite a chore even for the best of them.)

Good, I can see that several of you made a real effort to do a good job. It was rather difficult though, wasn't it? Now let me show you something. I can do it almost perfectly. (Use the ruler and draw a line. Then trace the letters from the plastic letter guide.)

There! How is that? It looks pretty good, doesn't it? What? Daniel says I cheated. No, I didn't cheat, but I'll tell you what I did do. I knew that drawing a straight line and making perfect letters was going to be a very hard job, and I knew that if I were going to do it right I would need a guide that was perfect, so I got one. As you can see from the paper, as long as I follow my perfect guide, my work will turn out rather well.

The same thing is true in other areas of life. There are lots of times when we need a guide. Can some of you think of times when we might need some guidance? (Several offers will be made such as trips, when we are lost, etc.) Yes, we could sure use a guide in all those cases. What about when we are trying to make difficult decisions? Sometimes we could really use a lot of help there, couldn't we? In fact, that is when we *really* need a *perfect* guide—one who can show us how to act and how to feel, someone who can show us the way we should treat other people. Do you know where we could find a perfect guide like that? That is what Jesus was and still is if we follow him.

That is also why we need to read our Bibles and talk to God in prayer each day. You see, if we never check the line we draw against the line we make using the ruler, we might never know when our line is off. So this week let's give some thought to what kind of things we do and say, and let's compare them to the perfect guide we have in Jesus. We know for sure that if we follow his example and do it in his Spirit we can't go wrong.

THE UNSEEN POWER

Text: *John 3:8. The wind blows where it wills, and you hear the sound of it, but you do not know whence it comes or whither it goes; so it is with every one who is born of the Spirit.*

Object: *Picture of a sailing ship in full sail.*

Main Thrust: *Some of the most powerful forces cannot be seen, but they are very real.*

I have a coloring book here. Can any of you tell me what it's about? Right! Pirates! I'll bet some of you would like to color in that one. There is one picture I especially want you to look at. This one. Can everyone see it? It is a picture of a big pirate ship with all the sails stretched out full. It's really cutting through the water! I have another picture here of several ships. See, here is an entire fleet moving across the ocean. We all know, of course, that sailing ships went all over the world. They still do, don't they? The question I would like to ask you is How? What made them move? They didn't have any motors. What made them go? Wind? Oh, is that the answer? You say, "Of course."

Now I want to ask you one more question. What is wind? (Let the children wrestle with it for a while, and do not accept half answers that are really not answers at all.) I can't see the wind. (Let them give a few more tries at explaining, then move on.)

Well, our main thought this morning is not to define wind, but rather to try to show you something. We all *know* the wind is there even if we can't see it or think of a way just off hand of defining it. We know it is there just like the sailors know. They know as soon as the wind stops, too. That is when everything stands still.

Did you know that that is similar to the way God works with us? Many times in the Bible, God's Holy Spirit is compared to a wind that blows. We can't see it with our eyes, but we can see the great things that happen when it comes, like a great fleet of sailing ships moving across the sea. We don't *see* the wind, but we know it is there.

God sends his Spirit like he sends the wind. It guides us and gives us the power to get where we need to go. Let's not worry about not seeing it, let's simply be glad that it is there and use it to do our very best.

44

OUTSIDE PRESSURE

Text: *Romans 12:1-2. I appeal to you therefore, brethren, by the mercies of God, to present your bodies as a living sacrifice, holy and acceptable to God, which is your spiritual worship. Do not be conformed to this world but be transformed by the renewal of your mind, that you may prove what is the will of God, what is good and acceptable and perfect.*

Object: *Some clay and clay molds.*

Main Thrust: *Being squeezed into a mold by other people.*

This morning I have a large lump of clay. How many of you have played with clay before, will you hold up your hands please? Oh, that's good. All of you know how much fun it is to make things out of clay then. In fact, we can shape this clay into just about anything we want it to be, can't we? What are some of the things you would like to make from this clay? (Let each child offer a suggestion before you do anything. It gives them a great feeling of being included, especially if they suggest an idea that you can pick up on and use as the actual illustration.)

Those are all good ideas. Do you think this piece of clay could really become all those things if we wanted it too? Of course it could. All right, then lets make some of them. (Get out your mold and place it in front of you.) First of all we are going to make an elephant. That was Nikki's idea. We'll just take the clay and press it into this mold here and—it's a horse! That's not what we wanted was it? I'll just add a little clay for a trunk and some more to the middle. Maybe then he will look more like an elephant. Now, let me see how it works. (Press it into the mold again.) Well, look at that, it came out looking like a horse again. How do you figure that? (Let the children provide the answers.)

What? The mold is shaped like a horse? Oh, I don't think that has anything to do with it. Let's try again. This time we can use David's suggestion. We will make a boat. All right, that is enough clay for a good-looking boat. Now we will just set it in the mold here and—look at that! It's a horse again! I don't understand it. Everything that gets close to that mold comes out looking like a horse. Can any of you explain it? (Let the children explain the process of clay molds.)

I see. In other words, if we squeeze the clay into the mold hard enough it will always come out looking the same, no matter what we wanted it to be. Do you want to know something interesting? The same thing is true with people. The apostle Paul once warned folks about being squeezed into molds. He knew that the world wants us to act in a certain way, and there will always be pressure on us, trying to push us into that mold.

For example, we know that Jesus would not want us to gossip or say unkind things about other people, but then we get in a group and they all begin talking and pretty soon we feel the pressure to join in. We feel like we need to say something too. That is when we are being squeezed into the mold.

We know that Jesus wants us to help others with our money, but we see everyone else buying candy and they look at us like we are a little strange if we say we are saving our money to help someone, so we buy it too. That's being pressed into the mold. It happens to us all of our lives, wherever we are. You will find that people are not nearly as interested in doing what is right as they are in doing what will gain approval. That's being pressed into the mold.

We have one advantage, however. Do you know what that is? As Christians, we follow Jesus first. If we keep looking at him, and following his actions, then we won't get pressed in so easily. He is our guide, and he is the one we follow. Watch him carefully, and when you feel the pressure to do something other than his will, ask for his help. Then you will know how really strong he is.

DEAD OR ALIVE

Text: *Matthew 23:27-28. Woe to you, scribes and Pharisees, hypocrites! for you are like whitewashed tombs, which outwardly appear beautiful, but within they are full of dead men's bones and all uncleaness. So you also outwardly appear righteous to men, but within you are full of hypocrisy and iniquity.*

Object: *Stuffed animals.*

Main Thrust: *Just because something looks alive on the outside doesn't mean it's alive on the inside.*

How many of you know what a taxidermist is? Does anyone know? (Take time for some fun guesses from the children.) Well, he is a man who stuffs dead animals and makes them look like they did when they were alive. I'm sure many of you have been to big museums where they have stuffed foxes or elephants. You may have been in someone's home and seen a fish or a deer head mounted on the wall. I have with me today a fish, he's really a big one isn't he? I didn't catch him, but I am told he put up quite a fight. He was very strong. You can see from the way he looks how solid and heavy he was.

What I want you to do is take a very close look at

48

him. When you do, you will see that he really looks exactly as he did when he was alive. His scales are all in the right order, his fins and tail look very powerful, his eyes are open. Even his teeth are in good condition. In fact, if you were to put him in the water he would look just like the live fish. There would only be one difference. Can you tell me what it is? Right! He's *not* alive. There is no life on the inside. No matter how good he *looks*, he is still dead.

Let me share one more thought with you. Sometimes people are much like this fish. I'm not talking about dead people who are stuffed like mummies. I am talking about people who are dead spiritually. Jesus came to show us how to live in a way that would make our lives worthwhile, both to ourselves and to others. How many of you can remember some afternoon or maybe a Saturday when you wanted to play and have fun but somehow nothing seemed to be what you really wanted to do? Can all of you think of a day like that? Sure you can. Someone would say let's play hide and seek or let's play cowboys, but nothing sounded like any fun. So it was a miserable day, wasn't it?

Now if someone were watching you, they would only see the outside of you. They would say "There's a fellow just like everyone else," just like this stuffed fish looks like other fish. But *you* know you feel bad inside. That is what Jesus was concerned about. He said that too often we worry about the *outside*—how we look or what others think about us—and we forget that it's what is inside that counts.

It is not enough for a Christian to *look* the part or to

go through all the right motions. We have to be alive on the inside and really make Jesus a part of us to be alive and enjoy the life he has for us.

This week, then, let's not be interested in simply looking the part, let's honestly try to *be* what Jesus wants. Let's make his Spirit of helping others, of sharing, of being thankful all a part of how we think and act. That way we stay alive on the inside as well as the outside. We sure don't want to be like a stuffed fish.

SQUEEZING IT OUT

Text: *Matthew 7:12. So whatever you wish that men would do to you, do so to them; for this is the law and the prophets.*

Object: *Sponge and a bowl of water.*

Main Thrust: *You have to squeeze the sponge to get anything out of it.*

Have all of you seen one of these before? It is a sponge. Do you know what sponges are used for? (Allow the children time to offer several suggestions.) That's right. We can use them to wash the car, wash dishes, even take a bath. But do you know why we can use sponges for all these things? Right! They soak up water. That's what I want you to see. I am going to set this sponge in a bowl of water and watch what happens. When I set it down it begins to absorb the water. Can you see how the water level is going down on the side of the bowl?

Now we have a sponge full of water. What do you think the sponge is going to do now? (Get some suggestions.) Well, I'll tell you—nothing! That's right, it's just going to set there and soak up more water. Once the water is taken in, that's where it stays until someone squeezes it out. As nice as sponges are, they only take things in, and they don't give them out until they're squeezed.

That may be a good quality in a sponge, but do you know there are some people who are the same way? They always seem to be around to soak things up, but they never want to share of themselves or give anything back. They are willing to have other people help them, but they won't help anyone else unless someone squeezes them a little. They are the people who like to think that everyone else owes them something and ought to be doing things just for them. We might call that kind of a person a sponge. They keep taking and taking, but they never give until they have to.

This week, while we are at school or out playing let's not only watch our friends, but also ourselves. Are we willing to share with others, or do we wait until we have to, until we are squeezed? Are we willing to wait for our turn, or do we try to rush to the front? Do we go out of our way to help even the people we don't like very much? Or do we just ignore them?

Jesus says we should go around *looking* for opportunities to help and that we should do the same thing for others that we would like them to do for us. In other words, we can't be a sponge and just soak things up and then hold them until we are squeezed. We are called to share freely because that's how God loves us.

UNDERSTANDING WHAT WE HEAR

Text: *Matthew 6:6. But when you pray, go into your room and shut the door and pray to your Father who is in secret; and your Father who sees in secret will reward you.*

Object: *Telegraph key.*

Main Thrust: *We hear what we listen for.*

I have something here you may have never seen before, but you have probably heard about. It's called a telegraph key. Listen carefully. (Send a short message on your key. It is not necessary to actually know Morse code although a few simple words could be easily memorized.) Now I am finished. Let's listen again. (Have an unseen accompanist return the message. You may "talk" back and forth for a few minutes. If you go longer than that however the children begin to lose interest.)

All right, who can tell me what they heard? David, what did you hear? A lot of clicks? Is that all? What did some of the rest of you hear? (Let several of them answer.) That is really amazing! All of you were right here, yet while you just heard a lot of clicking sounds, I heard a friend talking to me. He told me he likes me and gave me some help I needed to solve a problem. Why is it that none of you heard those things? Right!

You didn't know the code. That really makes all the difference, doesn't it?

Do you know that the same thing is true about God talking to us. No, he doesn't talk in code, but he does talk to us. The problem is we aren't training ourselves to listen. Lots of times Christians need guidance or help from God, and we pray and receive an answer. We say in prayer that we talk with God, and we do. Sometimes we hear God's answer in one way and sometimes we hear it in another. But the reason we can hear it is because we have trained ourselves to listen, just like I have trained myself to listen to the telegraph. Other people might say there was nothing there, but I know there was. Where they just heard clicking, I heard a friend. When they can't hear anything we can hear a great deal, because we are in the habit of listening. Would you like to know how to develop that habit a little more? Good. This week I would like you to try something.

(1) Say your prayers every *morning*. That's right. When you first get up, start off the day by asking God to help you be more like Jesus.

(2) Then spend some time, just a few seconds, being quiet. You know, when we talk to a friend we have to give him a chance to answer.

(3) Then, during the day, whenever you have a decision to make, no matter how large or small, ask yourself what Jesus would do. Then trust your conscience, that little voice inside. Many times that is how God talks to us. The more we listen, the better we get at hearing. The more we turn

him off, the more we become like those who can't hear at all. Then soon the message will come to us over and over, (send out some words on the telegraph key while you are explaining), but none of us will pay any attention. Let's not let that happen to us.

BLACK AND WHITE

Text: *Romans 10:12-13. For there is no distinction between Jew and Greek; the same Lord is Lord of all and bestows his riches upon all who call upon him. For, "every one who calls upon the name of the Lord will be saved."*

Object: *A piece of plain white paper, a piece of plain black paper, and a piece of paper with a message typed on it.*

Main Thrust: *People of different skin colors can work together to accomplish positive goals.*

How many of you can read? Will you hold up your hands please. Oh, that's good. I need some readers this morning. As you can see, I have three sheets of paper. Daniel, would you please read this one out loud to the group. (Hand him the clean white sheet of paper.) Would you go ahead and read that please. (Give him time to state his protest that the paper is blank.) Blank? It is not blank. There is a very important message written on it. Look again and see what you can find. (You may want to encourage his search over and over again.)

Let me have the paper, please. I'll take a look at it. Oh, I know what the problem is. Do any of you know? I wrote the ⋅message with *white* ink. White ink on

56

white paper. That doesn't work very well does it? What do we need? Right! We need some black ink. Here, let me give you this other sheet to read. (Hand him the piece of black paper.) That's a lot better, isn't it? Now we have the black ink. (As soon as they see it the children will point out the problem.)

You mean if its *all* black, we have the same problem as if it's *all* white? What can we do? Mix them! You mean have them work together and cooperate? The black letter and the white paper? When they work together it does make things a lot easier, doesn't it?

You know what? The same thing is true with people. Some folks think that its best if all white people are in one place and all black people are in another. I don't believe that's true. I think God wants all of us to learn to work together so we can accomplish things for him. We are all his children and we should love one another as much as he loves each of us.

IT'S GOING TO MELT!

Text: *Exodus 16:16-20. This is what the Lord has commanded: "Gather of it, every man of you, as much as he can eat; you shall take an omer apiece, according to the number of the persons whom each of you has in his tent." And the people of Israel did so; they gathered, some more, some less. But when they measured it with an omer, he that gathered much had nothing over, and he that gathered little had no lack; each gathered according to what he could eat. And Moses said to them, "Let no man leave any of it till the morning." But they did not listen to Moses; some left part of it till the morning, and it bred worms and became foul; and Moses was angry with them.*

Object: *An ice cream cone and a towel.*

Main Thrust: *We should learn to enjoy life and not try to save everything.*

(This talk is a lot of fun because it deals directly with a problem all children have: eating a melting cone. You may have an accomplice keep the cone in the church refrigerator until shortly before the talk begins. The softer the ice cream is, the better. You want it to be melting during the talk—so the towel is essential!)

We are really going to have some fun this morning.

Can you guess what we are going to talk about? I'll tell you—no, I'll show you. Patti is bringing it down the aisle now.That's right, an ice cream cone. (You can have the towel in your lap while she comes down the aisle. Accept the cone and continue.) Thank you, Patti. That is a good-looking ice cream cone, isn't it? Boy, I bet it will taste good. Have any of you ever had one like this? (Allow for answers. The more enthusiasm that can be built toward eating the cone the better.)

Your comments have made me hungry. I really am anxious to see how it tastes. (Take a small bite.) Oh, that's *great*! In fact, its so good, do you know what I'm going to do? I'm going to save it until later and eat it then. I'll just set it here on the towel, and after the service I will eat it. What do you think of that idea?

David says it won't work. Why not? If it's good I ought to save it right? Daniel says it will melt. You mean it won't keep? What should I do? Right, eat it now. That really does seem like a logical thing to do. Don't you think so?

But may I tell you a secret? Lot's of people don't know that it's all right to enjoy things now. Every time something good or fun happens they think they ought to store it away for sometime in the future. The trouble is, it seems to melt away and they *never* get to enjoy it. Jesus said he came to give us an abundant life. A happy life in him. He said it is all right to take life one day at a time and really enjoy it.

So the next time you are in a situation where people tell you not to enjoy things or try to save all the good things, remember the ice cream cone. If I eat it now I can enjoy it. If I try to save it, all I'll have is a puddle. Do you know what I'm going to do? Right! I'm going to enjoy it. I hope all of you enjoy each minute of the day as much as I am going to enjoy eating this ice cream cone.

HARDENING OUR HEARTS

Text: *II Kings 17:13-14. Yet the Lord warned Israel and Judah by every prophet and every seer, saying, "Turn from your evil ways and keep my commandments and my statutes, in accordance with all the law which I commanded your fathers, and which I sent to you by my servants the prophets." But they would not listen, but were stubborn, as their fathers had been, who did not believe in the Lord their God.*

Object: *A thick callus or some part of your hand or arm and a needle.*

Main Thrust: *If we work long enough, we can become callous to feeling God's prodings.*

I would like you to watch something very carefully this morning. Do you see what I have in my hand? Right. It is a long pin. Will some of you touch the end of it with your finger please. Be careful, its sharp. (Let several of the children touch it.) There, that's good. Now, watch carefully because I am going to stick this pin into my knuckle. (Select a callus somewhere on your hand, then stick the pin straight in. Do not slip it sideways through the surface layer of dead skin. The children have all seen that done a hundred times by other children. Put the pin straight in and leave it.

The callus will hold it and the children will be fascinated.)

There. You see how it works? Do you know why I can do that and not feel it? Because I have a callus there. A callus is a place where the skin has gotten so thick or dead that the nerves don't feel things anymore. I got these two calluses on my knuckles from practicing karate every day. We start out striking soft things, then slowly the callus builds so that we can strike very hard things, and it doesn't hurt because the nerves are dead and there is no feeling. See, that pin is still sticking right into the knuckle. I don't want you to try it, just look at it.

Do you want to know something important? Jesus talked about calluses too. He was a strong carpenter, and he had spent a lot of time working with rough wood and logs. Jesus had plenty of calluses, a lot more than I do. But there was one kind that worried him. Do you know what it was? It was the kind of callus we get on our hearts.

No, we don't get thick skin on our hearts, but we do get something that makes them insensitivie. You remember I said that in karate we start out by hitting soft things, then build up to hard objects? Well, the same is true with our hearts. We don't start right out very hard hearted, we develop over a period of time. First we say no to God on just the little things. For example, we know we ought to go to Sunday school, but it sure feels good to stay in bed. The first time it is a little bit of a struggle to stay there, but we do, then we notice that the next time it is a little easier and a little easier. The callus is forming. After a while, we don't have the desire to get up and go at all.

That can be true of every part of our life. It happens the first time we see someone who needs our help, but we decide we would rather play. We feel badly about it for a while, but pretty soon we forget. Then we see someone else who needs help, but this time it's a little bit easier to turn them down. The callus is forming. After a while, things that would have really made us feel bad once, are just like this pin is now to me. It's there, and its sharp, but my callus is so thick I don't feel it.

This week, let's do some thinking about our hearts and the kind of calluses we may be building. When we see someone who needs our help, let's help, not shut him out. When we see a chance to do something good, let's do it. That way we keep the doors open and the calluses off. We may end up with tender hearts, but we will have happy ones.

GIVE AN INCH

Text: *Luke 11:24-26. When the unclean spirit has gone out of a man, he passes through waterless places seeking rest; and finding none he says, "I will return to my house from which I came." And when he comes he finds it swept and put in order. Then he goes and brings seven other spirits more evil than himself, and they enter and dwell there; and the last state of that man becomes worse than the first.*

Object: *Piano bench.*

Main Thrust: *If we keep giving a little ground long enough, we will give up all of it.*

I would like all of you to come over by the piano with me for a few minutes. You can all sit on the front pews, except for Daniel. I would like him to sit here on the very end of the piano bench, and no matter what happens I want him to stay on the bench. Now we are going to say that Daniel is a very good Christian. He is doing what Jesus asked him to do and enjoying life. Then one day a little thing called temptation comes along. Just a little one; about the size of Nikki (choose one of the smallest children). Nikki, would you come up and sit next to Daniel. (Let her come to the end of the bench on which Daniel is seated so that he will

64

have to move slightly toward the center of the bench to make room for her.) That wasn't so bad. He let in one little temptation, but there is still plenty of room on the bench.

Now what would happen if just one more little temptation came and he begun thinking about it. He may say, "Last time nothing happened, I'll let in just one more." Patti, would you come and sit next to Nikki please. (Have Patti sit next to Nikki. This should push the first child to the center of the bench.) As you continue to talk about the "little" temptations, call other children to slide onto the bench. In a matter of minutes Daniel should be sitting on the floor.

What happened, Daniel? Why are you standing over there? You are supposed to be on the bench. I guess it got a little crowded didn't it?" All right you may all sit down now. Did all of you see what happened to poor Daniel? (Allow the children time to laugh and share some comments.)

Do you know what I am trying to show you this morning? It is important, because the same thing that happened to Daniel here today can happen to each one of us if we are not careful. We all try to be Christians, and that means we believe certain things and try to act the way Jesus acted. Many times, however, we begin to think that if we got along with a little temptation once or if we do something wrong just one time it won't be any problem. Then we do it once more and once more and—. You remember what happened to Daniel. He just gradually got pushed off the bench.

This week let's think about how many times we let

one little wrong thought or action come and sit next to us, and when we see it there let's throw it out quickly before it invites some friends. Once they start moving in, we may find that we are being pushed right off the bench.

God loves us and he will give us all the help we need. All we have to do is make up our mind that we will work with God and keep the temptations from getting too comfortable. Like the man who swept out his house, once we get them out, we don't want them coming back. Let's really work on that one.

WORKING TOGETHER

Text: *I Corinthians 2:5-9. That your faith might not rest in the wisdom of men but in the power of God. Yet among the mature we do impart wisdom, although it is not a wisdom of this age or of the rulers of this age, who are doomed to pass away. But we impart a secret and hidden wisdom of God, which God decreed before the ages for our glorification. None of the rulers of this age understood this; for if they had, they would not have crucified the Lord of glory. But, as it is written,*

> *"What no eye has seen, nor ear heard,*
> *nor the heart of man conceived,*
> *what God has prepared for those who love him."*

Object: *Piano harmony.*

Main Thrust: *Everyone has an important function in the whole plan.*

(If the pastor does not play the piano he can do this in cooperation with the pianist.) Can everyone see what I have here? That's right. It is a hymnbook. As you can see, I have it open to one of the hymns. We sang it today. If you look closely, you will see that there are lots of little black spots on the lines of each page. Those are called notes. Each black note represents a key on the piano. That is how the pianist knows which key to play. Now I am going to sit down at the piano and play one of these hymns for you. Gather around and tell me if the sounds are familiar. You all know this hymn. (Pick one that is well known in your congregation. Then proceed to play the base line by itself. Of course, no one will recognize it.)

There! Did you enjoy that? Who can tell me what it was? No one? I'm really disappointed. No one knew it. I'll bet I know why. I just played the bottom line. Let me play the next line, the tenor line. Then you'll all know. (When you finish that one you should, of course, receive the same responses.)

This is really something. Let's try the alto line. (Begin playing, but stop after a few measures.) I can see no one knows that either. I guess these lines are really useless. Let's skip all those and play the melody line. (Play a few measures, that's all it should take.) There, that's better. Now you all know what we are playing. I guess this top line is really the important one. It is the one that fits the words. Listen to how pretty it is. (Play the melody line through once.) Now, that really sounds the way it should, didn't it? (Let some of the children reflect. They will know something is wrong and that it sounds too thin, but they may not be sure how to express it. Let them try. In a few seconds someone will come up with it or at least be close enough that you can pick up on it.)

That's right. It still doesn't sound like it should does it? What do you think we ought to do? Right! Let's add the lines we took out. The ones we said weren't important. (Play the song through in full harmony.) There! That sounds much better. I guess those other lines were important after all. We won't make that mistake again. Next time we will use all the notes.

You know, it might be a good idea to use the same approach with people who seem to stand out, the ones who sing the melody. We forget that *everyone* is important, no matter what part they play. Every person needs the help of others. That means everyone here this morning has an important part to play. You may say that none of us here stands out like a melody, but you remember how thin the melody sounded without the help of all those other lines. Always remember that you are important, because God has given you your talent and abilities. If they weren't important He wouldn't have given you the command to use them.

This week I would like each of you to think about the many things you can do, and how you can use them to help God and others.

DOING THE WRONG THING
THE RIGHT WAY

Text: *Matthew 15:14. Let them alone; they are blind guides. And if a blind man leads a blind man, both will fall into a pit.*

Object: *Pictures to copy—simple with few lines, a few lines of numbers, pads, and pencils.*

Main Thrust: *If you copy the wrong thing the right way, your copy is right, you just have the wrong guide.*

Do all of you have a pencil and paper? Good! This morning we are not going to take a test, but I would like you to draw something for me. If you will look carefully you will see that I have a design drawn on this large paper. What I would like you to do is copy this design that I have as carefully as you can. All right, go ahead and copy it. (Give them plenty of time so that the younger ones will be able to finish. Be sure to give pencils and paper even to the *very* youngest, otherwise they will feel left out. In the same manner the pencils should be large enough for little fingers to control and the design kept very simple, like a square.)

All right, now that we've all had plenty of time, let's see how well you draw. I want all of your designs to look like a triangle. (Hold up another piece of paper with a triangle on it. The children will put up quite a protest when you hold up a different paper. Let them go ahead and complain for a few seconds.)

Now you are telling me that you copied the design all right, but I gave you the wrong design to follow. Is that right? I see. So the problem is not that you are bad artists, in fact you are good artists. You followed the design you had very well. But it was the *wrong* design. It is possible then to be a good artist and have a wrong design. That is very interesting.

I want you to think about that this week because the same thing that happened just now with the paper can happen with our lives. Did you know that? It's true. There will be lots of times when you will hear someone say, "Oh, he's a bad boy," or "She is a naughty girl." But that really isn't true. They might do something they shouldn't do, but that does not make them a bad boy or a naughty girl. Usually the fact is that we are being good and following bad examples. What we should strive for is a good example to use as a model. That is what God gave us in Jesus.

This week, just for fun, every time you have to make a decision, try taking Jesus as your example and see if you can copy his actions and attitudes. Then you will have a perfect picture to draw from, and your picture or actions will come out better.

IT WAS THERE ALL THE TIME

Text: *Matthew 9:9. As Jesus passed on from there, he saw a man called Matthew sitting at the tax office; and he said to him, "Follow me." And he rose and followed him.*

Object: *A piece of paper and a book on Japanese paper folding. (The book can be found in almost any library. An hour spent with such a book will be more than enough for the talk and also can prove to be a fascinating pastime.)*

Main Thrust: *The way something is folded brings out different things.*

How many of you can tell me what I have with me this morning? That's right. It is a piece of plain white paper. What else is it? Can anyone guess what else it can be? (Let them guess for a while. It is amazing what they can come up with. In this instance they may have some difficulty, however.)

A few of you have some ideas, but most of us just see a plain piece of white paper. Watch for just a second and I will show you something I think you may find interesting. If I fold this paper carefully in a few places—look! We have a bird, complete with flying wings. Did any of you see that in the paper? No? Let's try again. With just a few folds here and there, now we have—a flower. I'll bet you didn't see that either. Just for fun, let's try one more. If we make a few folds in other places, look now. Now we have a fish. How about that? Who would have thought that all these things could be in just a plain piece of white paper, yet with a little folding in the right places, there they were. From now on we will have to be more careful about referring to something as just a plain old piece of paper. Now that we know some of the things it can become with just a little help.

The important thing, however, is to realize that people are the same way. Lots of times we will see someone sitting off alone and we say, "Oh, that's just John. He's no fun." That is when we need to remember the paper. Maybe if we took the time to get to know him, he would turn out to be very interesting and lots of fun.

This week I would like you to try what I am talking about. When you are playing or when you're at school, try to find someone you think is dull or just plain old so-and-so and try to become friends with him. Talk to him and see what he is interested in, and how much fun he can be. I think you'll find that most people are like this paper. They look very plain until we learn how to draw things out of them. Then they can be lots of fun to know.

THE COMMON THREAD

Text: *I Corinthians 13:13. So faith, hope, love abide, these three; but the greatest of these is love.*

Object: *Beads and a string.*

Main Thrust: *Love holds things together.*

You can all see that I have a large cigar box with me today, but that is not our object. What we are going to talk about is on the inside. It's a whole box full of loose beads. Can you think of some things that we can do with these beads? (At this point let the children use their imaginations freely. They may suggest such things as a necklace, a ring, a bracelet, or pins, etc.)

Those are a lot of good suggestions. As you can all see, these loose beads can be turned into just about anything we want. But I'm not sure exactly how you could do that. Something else must be needed. You can't put a bunch of loose beads around your neck. What do you do about that?

Oh, you need to put a thread through the beads, something to bind them together. Then once we have a wire or a string, the beads stay together and they can do the job we intended. That is the vital factor: something to hold them next to one another. Very good!

The point I would like to make with you is that people are a lot like these beads. You can look at all these beads in the box, and you can see that they are all different sizes, shapes, and colors. It is not until they are bound together by something that they fulfill a greater purpose. If you turn around and look at the congregation you will see that, like the beads, there are people of all different sizes, colors, and shapes. We need something to bind people together too. Do you know what that something is? That's right, it's love. Our love for one another.

Jesus knew that all of us have a tendency to go our own way or to do just the things we want to do, so he tried to show us how to love and live our lives for others. That is what I would like you to think about this week. When you are at school and see someone sitting alone, remember the beads and let your love be like a string that draws that person into a group of new friends. When you hear someone saying something about another person, remember to look for the good things and keep your friendship strong. When you are playing, remember that we are all in the same game to have fun with one another and share the things you have. Each day, do something to make your love for other people stronger. Then, as a group, all working together we can really be God's church.

Remember, love is the string. If it breaks, the beads go in all different directions and we don't have much of anything left. It's our love that keeps that from happening.

OPENING DOORS

Text: *Proverbs 20:5. The purpose in a man's mind is like a deep water, but a man of understanding will draw it out.*

Object: *A doorknob and pictures of other types of knobs.*

Main Thrust: *There is something good in everybody if we only take time to get to know the way to open them up.*

I have something here that all of you have seen before. It is a doorknob. Can you all see it? Good. This is a plain doorknob, but there are lots of other types around. I'm sure you have seen many of them. Here are some pictures of all different types of knobs. There really are lots of them, aren't there?

I would like to tell you about something that happened to me as a little boy. When I was small, just before Christmas, my mother used to hide things in the closet. I knew they were in there, but I couldn't work the doorknob to get them out. No matter how hard I tried, I couldn't get the door open and get to the really good things. Then, slowly, I got bigger, and after a while I learned how to open doors with the doorknob—all different kinds of knobs and handles. Then I could get all the good things hidden away inside the closet. That was really great!

But, you know what else I learned and what I would like to share with you? I learned that people are a lot like my mother's closet. All of them have some really wonderful things inside of them, but many times we are unable to open the door and let it out. We have to find the knob and open them up. The thing we must remember is that there are lots of different knobs, like we saw in the picture. One of the fun things we do as Christians is to try to find the knob to open up each person we meet and find the really beautiful things inside. Jesus was a master at seeing inside people, and he always tried to bring out the very best. This week let's look for new handles to open up people we meet, and then enjoy all the good things we find inside them.

MAGIC WORDS

Text: *Matthew 7:12. So whatever you wish that men would do to you, do so to them; for this is the law and the prophets.*

Object: *A smile.*

Main Thrust: *People usually respond to us according to the way we treat them.*

How many of you know what magic is? Very good! How many of you can do magic? Ah, not so many. Well, this morning I am going to give you a lead on something that works very much like magic, and each one of you can do it. How would you like that?

Do you want to see someone change? Watch (Turn to one of the youngest children and smile with him for a few seconds. It shouldn't take much to get him laughing.) Look at that. He was so serious just a second ago, now look how happy he is. He has really changed. Look! There is another one. (Laughter is contagious among children, and it should not take long before the entire group is with you.)

Look how we have changed the entire group, just from one piece of magic: a smile. It really made things different didn't it? What do you think would happen if we spread that magic all over the church. (Let the answers flow freely, you may learn a great deal about the church.) Right! We could change everyone into a smiler. That would really be great. We will remember that.

Let me give you two more secrets before we go. One is the word *please*. I will bet that your parents have told you about that word before. Have you all heard it? Good! It really makes people feel that we care about them and we are not just ordering them around. No one likes to be treated that way.

The other magic word is *Thank you*. It is really a great word. It tells people that we truly appreciate what they have done for us. That makes them feel better, and they are more willing to help us again.

So you see, the words and a smile really are like magic. When we spread them around freely they make people feel better, and then we are all happy together!